What Is
Climate Change?

by Gail Herman

illustrated by John Hinderliter

Penguin Workshop
An Imprint of Penguin Random House

To Bennett and Sam, for their guidance
and inspiration—GH

For Keegan, because science is cool—JH

PENGUIN WORKSHOP
Penguin Young Readers Group
An Imprint of Penguin Random House LLC

Copyright © 2018 by Penguin Random House LLC. All rights reserved. Published by
Penguin Workshop, an imprint of Penguin Random House LLC, 345 Hudson Street,
New York, New York 10014. PENGUIN and PENGUIN WORKSHOP are trademarks
of Penguin Books Ltd. WHO HQ & Design is a registered trademark of
Penguin Random House LLC. Printed in the USA.

Library of Congress Cataloging-in-Publication Data is available.

ISBN 9781524786151 (paperback)   10 9 8 7 6 5 4 3
ISBN 9781524786175 (library binding)   10 9 8 7 6 5 4 3 2

Contents

What Is Climate Change?

In the Canadian Arctic, winter used to come early. By early November, temperatures dipped below zero. Snow covered the ground. Hudson Bay became covered in solid ice.

Hundreds of polar bears lumbered onto the frozen water, making their way out to open ocean. All winter long, they swam from ice floe to ice floe. They mated. They hunted and fished. There were plenty of ringed seals to eat.

When summer finally came in August, the ice melted. The polar bears swam back to land. The males play-fought. The females watched over their young cubs. Months passed. Polar bears lounged on tundra—still-frozen ground—using little energy. They waited for cold weather. They waited to go out to sea again.

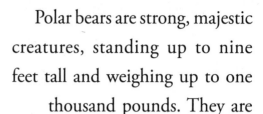

Polar bears are strong, majestic creatures, standing up to nine feet tall and weighing up to one thousand pounds. They are built for the cold. Their snow-white coat is thick, with a double layer of fur. Also, a layer of fat lies just under their skin, keeping them extra warm. For months, polar bears have to live off this fat, gained from winter feedings on the ice. When they're on land, they barely eat.

In early November 2016, the polar bears were still on land. There was no sea ice on Hudson Bay. Weeks passed. By December, there was still barely any ice at all. So the polar bears had to wait longer to return to the sea. Some paced back and forth along the shoreline. Others lay on the ground, not doing much at all.

The warmer climate affected the polar bears in important ways. In the 1980s, Hudson Bay bears were bigger and rounder, well fed. Recently they've been losing weight and becoming

Polar bear in Hudson Bay from the 1980s

weaker. That's because with fewer weeks on ice, their hunting season has become shorter. They have less food. In Hudson Bay, polar bear numbers have dropped. The bears have fewer cubs. And not all cubs survive.

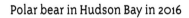

Polar bear in Hudson Bay in 2016

In 2016, the water in Hudson Bay didn't freeze until December 12. That was very late. "Sea ice is finally forming," one scientist reported. "The polar bears are moving quickly offshore."

Even on ice, however, the polar bears had a tougher time. There was more water between floes. The polar bears were already weakened by long months on land. And yet they had to swim longer distances to get from place to place to hunt.

Observers followed one female who had to swim nine days straight to reach an ice floe.

The Arctic—the polar bears' habitat—is changing. Temperatures have gone up about 3 degrees Celsius (°C), or 5.4 degrees Fahrenheit (°F), since 1900.

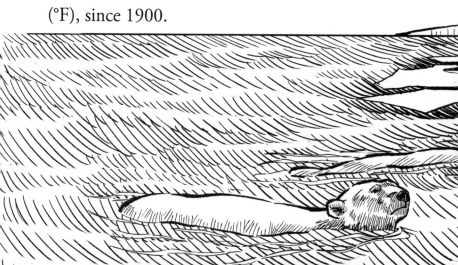

The ice cover is shrinking, too. In 2017, it was 30 percent smaller than it was twenty-five years earlier. And each year, the remaining ice cover is melting faster and faster.

The fact is that our entire planet is getting warmer, not just the Arctic. Certain gases in the atmosphere—"greenhouse gases"—hold in heat, keeping it from escaping into space. Higher temperatures bring changes in plant and animal life. In sources of food and water. In rainfall and snowfall, floods and droughts. Habitats around the world are at risk.

It's all part of climate change.

CHAPTER 1
Things Are Heating Up

First of all, what is climate?

Before you dress each day, do you check the climate to figure out what to wear? No, you check the weather.

Weather changes often, sometimes in the space of a couple of hours. Climate doesn't. Climate is the weather over long periods of time.

Scientists who study climate look at weather patterns. They need to measure temperature and precipitation (rainfall and snowfall). They'll look to see if there are changes over thirty years, fifty years, or even one hundred years. By studying these long periods, they see whether conditions on Earth are changing.

Scientists have taken measurements from weather stations around the world, in hot places and cold ones. And the average temperatures in all these places have gone up almost 2°F since the 1880s. That may not sound like a big difference, but it is.

Earth has been having fewer cold days and more warm days. There have been fewer record low temperatures and more record highs. Even freezing-cold places are getting warmer, and not just in the Arctic. It's also happening in Antarctica, by the South Pole. Ice caps, glaciers, and ice sheets—all forms of land ice—are melting.

Plateau Glacier circa 1961

· Plateau Glacier circa 2003

When land ice melts, it runs into the sea. The additional water from the Arctic Ocean ends up flowing into all the oceans. This causes sea levels to rise around the world. On average, levels have risen eight inches since the early 1900s and about two inches since 2000.

Again, that doesn't seem like much. But these changes in the Arctic have an impact on weather patterns for the entire planet. It's like a teeny, tiny spark that sets off a fire.

In Alaska, coastal villages have already seen dramatic change. Homes are threatened by flooding and erosion—that's water wearing away the shoreline. Sea ice is melting. So is permafrost,

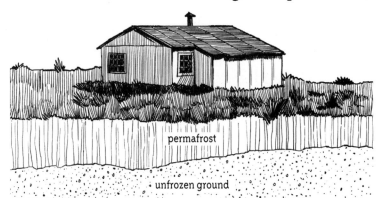

permafrost

unfrozen ground

the permanently frozen soil just under the ground. The permafrost even feels different. It's springy, which causes houses to collapse into the water.

The people of an island town called Shishmaref have voted to move their village. It will take years and much money to do it. But the people are ready. "The land is going away," one man explained.

What about places that are already hot? Higher temperatures are bringing changes in these areas, too. Land is drying out. Water sources are dwindling.

In Africa, Lake Chad sits on the edge of the Sahara Desert. Millions of people in Chad,

Cameroon, Nigeria, and Niger relied on the lake—once one of the largest in Africa—for drinking water, fishing, and farming. But there is hardly any lake left. Since 1963, Lake Chad has lost nearly 90 percent of its water. It has shrunk because higher temperatures made the water evaporate at a faster pace. (Overuse is another reason. After all, the lake provided food and water for so many.)

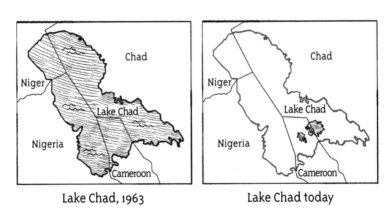

Lake Chad, 1963   Lake Chad today

So how do climate scientists explain this global warming? It all starts with greenhouse gases in our atmosphere.

CHAPTER 2
Something in the Air

Earth's atmosphere begins with the air surrounding the planet, and it stretches all the way out to space. (That's about sixty miles above Earth.) Our atmosphere is made up of layers of gases.

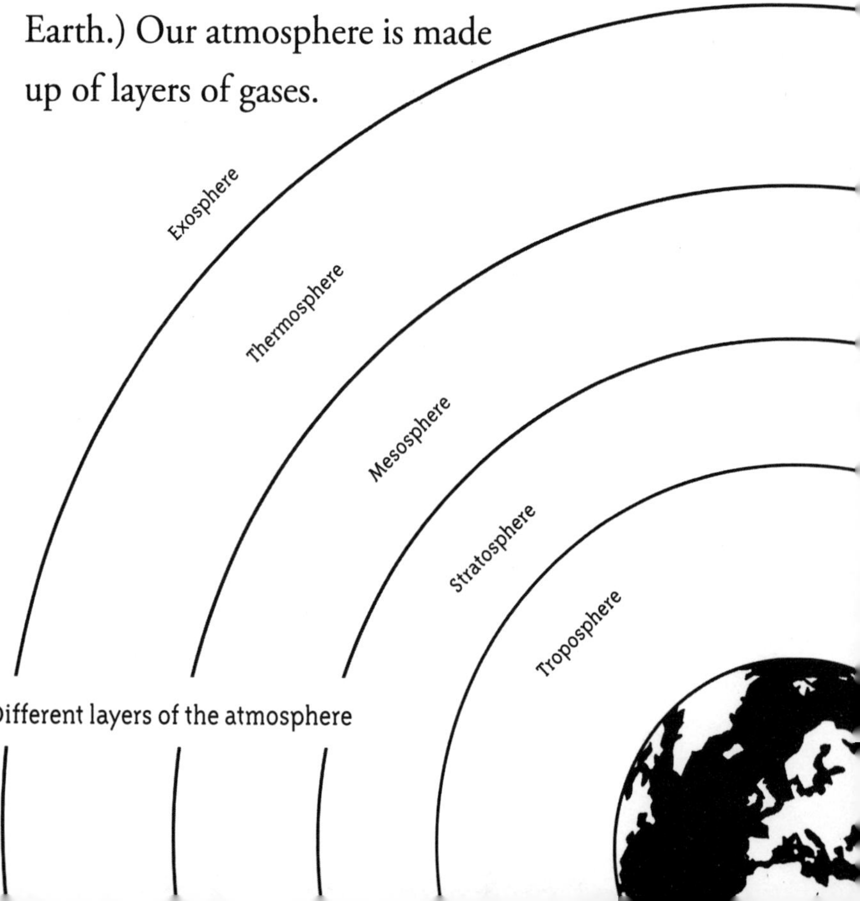

Exosphere

Thermosphere

Mesosphere

Stratosphere

Troposphere

Different layers of the atmosphere

Air has oxygen, of course. We need it to breathe. In fact, oxygen and another gas called nitrogen make up more than 99 percent of our atmosphere. That means only 1 percent of the atmosphere contains other gases. But it's those other gases that help control Earth's climate.

We can't see any of these gases. We can't smell them or taste them. But they help heat Earth in a way that's similar to how a greenhouse keeps plants warm. (That's why they're called greenhouse gases.) In a greenhouse, sunlight streams through the glass, warming everything inside.

Sunlight, a form of energy, streams through our atmosphere, too. Most of the energy is absorbed by Earth's surface. It warms up everything. But some of this energy bounces back into space. The heat escapes.

Greenhouse gases, however, can stop the heat from leaving. They trap it, like a blanket traps your body heat to keep you warm at night. Without greenhouse gases, the planet would be a cold, lifeless place.

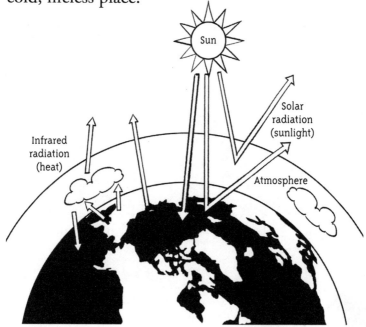

For the last ten thousand years, these gases have helped keep Earth's temperature steady. (An average global temperature that's in the high fifties Fahrenheit is perfect for animals and plants to grow.)

But Earth set new records for highest-ever global temperatures three years in a row: 2014, 2015, and 2016. And between 2001 and 2016, Earth had sixteen of the seventeen warmest years on record dating back to 1880.

If greenhouse gases have always been part of our atmosphere, why is Earth getting warmer now?

It's because, in recent years, greenhouse gas levels have risen. And one gas in particular is trapping more and more heat. It's called carbon dioxide, or CO_2 for short.

CO_2 is made up of oxygen and one other element: carbon. (An element is something so simple, it can't be broken into smaller substances.)

Like oxygen, carbon is everywhere. It is in every form of life—and in oceans, rocks, and soil. It moves from living things to the environment, then back to living things.

How does this cycle work?

People and animals breathe in oxygen and breathe out CO_2. Plants and trees take in CO_2 to grow and make food. In the process, they emit—send out—oxygen.

It's like a delicate balancing act. But more CO_2 in the air throws things off balance. It causes climate change.

Of course, climate change isn't something that started only recently. It's happened again and again, over the course of billions of years.

CHAPTER 3
Climate Change through the Ages

Hothouse. Icehouse. Snowball. These three terms have all described Earth.

At times, over the course of billions of years,

the planet has been a hothouse, with much warmer temperatures than we have now. It's been too warm for any glaciers or ice sheets to form.

At other times, Earth has been an icehouse, cold enough to create much larger glaciers and vaster ice sheets. The planet has even been a "Snowball Earth," covered almost completely with ice, slush, and snow.

Learning about Past Climates

Scientists use different methods to figure out what the climate on Earth was like hundreds, thousands, and even millions of years ago:

- They examine tree rings, the "growth bands" that develop within tree trunks. The rings are wider in warm years and thinner in cold ones.

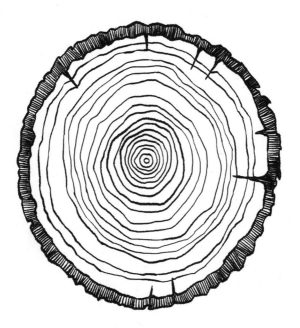

- They look at coral reefs that are millions of years old. Reefs have growth bands, plus they hold a form of oxygen that helps measure long-ago ocean temperatures.

- They analyze ancient shells, buried deep in the ocean, that contain the same form of oxygen as coral does.
- They also drill deep into glacial ice cores to get samples of ancient ice. Tiny air bubbles trapped inside tell scientists about CO_2 levels and temperature.

In the beginning, 4.6 billion years ago when Earth first formed, it was at its absolute hottest. The temperature was likely more than 3,600°F. Scientists are still learning about young Earth.

First, it is supposed that a giant cloud of gas and dust spun through space. Rocks, dust, and gas collided. Gravity kept these bits and pieces together. The "chunks" grew larger and rounder, forming Earth and the other planets in our solar system. They all circled a much bigger glowing ball of gas: the sun.

All those space collisions created great heat. Earth was too hot to have a solid surface. Instead, "seas" of melted rock covered the planet.

Hundreds of millions of years passed. Earth cooled. The planet shifted a bit. It traveled around the sun at a slightly different angle. Because of this, Earth began to have seasons. Rain fell. Oceans formed. Earth cooled even more. Masses of land developed, along with volcanoes.

Volcanoes and Climate

Volcanoes release CO_2 during eruptions and also from underground melted rock that seeps through cracks. Compared to millions of years ago, there is much less volcanic activity today. Yet erupting volcanoes still affect climate. Spewing ash forms a haze that blocks sunlight, causing a temporary cooling. The ash clears within a few years. But the volcano's CO_2—and its warming effect—lasts much longer.

At that point, Earth was still very hot; most likely more than 400°F. Humans couldn't have survived. Also, the atmosphere had no oxygen.

Still, one simple form of life did develop: a kind of bacteria living in oceans. The bacteria gave off oxygen, so Earth had the beginnings of breathable air, making way for different forms of life.

Then the climate changed. A Snowball Earth developed. Maybe all that new oxygen replaced

Snowball Earth

greenhouse gases, cooling the planet. Or maybe there was a lull in volcanic activity, reducing CO_2. Either way, scientists have found glacial rocks and other evidence of ice in every corner of the world, from the North Pole to the South Pole, and from South Asia to South America.

Then, over more time, underwater volcanoes built up under the ice. Again they spewed gases through cracks. They became more and more active. New forms of life developed around them. These creatures breathed in oxygen and released CO_2. This caused Earth to thaw out over hundreds of millions of years.

Sponges growing around the base of underwater volcanoes.

Two more deep freezes followed, ending about 550 million years ago. Was Earth finished changing? No. Land shifted and collided. New oceans formed. More volcanoes formed. More eruptions followed.

The temperature climbed and climbed. About 540 million years ago, it may have reached an average global high of 90°F—around thirty degrees warmer than the average is today.

Meanwhile, more life was developing—plants and trees, and animals. With each shift in climate, new species developed. Others died out.

Then came the Age of the Dinosaurs. It lasted until 66 million years ago. Earth had a warm, wet climate without any polar ice caps or glaciers. Forests grew close to both the North and South Poles. The CO_2 level was five times greater than it is today.

The Dinosaur Age ended with another major change in climate. One theory is that an asteroid or comet struck Earth. It moved great masses of land. It buried plants and animals. Wildfires raged, and soot and dust filled the air, blocking the sun for several years. Earth became cold and dark. The dinosaurs were wiped out.

Slowly, the air cleared. Temperatures warmed and kept warming. By then, our continents were all in place. Small, mouselike mammals evolved. And still the planet got warmer.

Eventually, around 56 million years ago, Earth grew so hot that palm trees and crocodiles lived above the Arctic Circle.

However, for the last two million years or so—from the time some of our earliest human ancestors walked the Earth to today—the climate on Earth has been in a pretty steady state.

That does not mean there haven't been any further climate changes. It means the planet settled into natural climate cycles. (A cycle is a series of events that repeat in the same order.) And Earth has had regular cycles of warm and cool climates, with each cycle lasting about one hundred thousand years.

Woolly mammoth

When you hear the term "Ice Age," you probably think of the most recent one—a cold, frozen time that ended about twelve thousand years ago. Animals like the woolly mammoth and saber-toothed cats were alive.

Saber-toothed cat

One well-known idea suggested that during this time, modern humans first traveled to North America, crossing a land bridge from what is now the region of Russia known as Siberia. This bridge was made possible by shallow seas, a consequence of low temperatures. However, new studies seem to disprove this theory.

Back then, average temperatures were 5–15°F

colder than now. In some places, even summer felt like winter. And ice sheets reached all the way to what is now New York City. Humans wore layers and layers of animal fur to stay warm.

But even ice ages have cold *and* warm climates. That sounds confusing, but it is true.

A lot depends on Earth's orbit, the way it circles the sun. Sometimes during an ice age, the shape of Earth's orbit keeps it farther from the sun year-round, and the climate grows colder. These times are called glacial periods.

When Earth's orbit changes shape, bringing it closer to the sun, the planet warms. These times are known as interglacial periods. (*Inter* is from Latin and it means "between.")

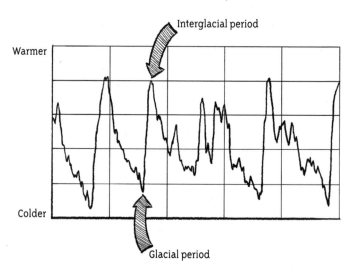

Believe it or not, right now, we're in a warm interglacial period of an ice age. Scientists disagree exactly when the next cold glacial period might occur.

But well-known climate expert Dr. Joseph Romm has written that he and the "world's top scientists have confidence" that right now, the long-term trend for Earth—"driven largely by changes in our orbit"—should be "a very slow cooling."

Dr. Joseph Romm

Earth should be cooling. Not warming the way it is. So something clearly seems off.

Also, another weird thing is happening. In the past, each of the climate shifts took place slowly over millions of years. This time, everything is happening much quicker. It's almost like pressing a fast-forward button.

How do climate scientists explain all that?

CHAPTER 4
The Change Begins

Nearly all—97 percent—of climate scientists agree: Humans, and their impact on the Earth, are making the difference.

The principal geologist at the British Geological Survey explained, "We have had an incredible impact on the environment of our planet." Another geology professor later added, "We . . . are just realizing the scale and permanence of the change."

Recent human activity is the reason why Earth is warming and also why it's happening at such a rapid rate. (Some feel we should even mark this as a new era, much like the Age of the Dinosaurs: the Age of Humans.)

Recent human activity refers to the past

200–250 years, when technology began hugely changing the way people live.

It all began with a revolution, although one that wasn't a war. The Industrial Revolution was a time of new ideas and new inventions.

In the United States, it started in the late 1700s with one cotton mill in Rhode Island. More factories followed.

Earlier, mostly everything had been made or built in homes or small workshops. People spun their own thread, sewed their own clothes, and made their own candles.

With new machinery, production (which means making things) shifted to large, shared spaces: factories. These factories were powered by

coal. They produced large amounts of goods—fast. It became easier to buy factory-made items—clothes, for instance—than to sew them by hand.

Soon, factory-made gas lamps replaced homemade candles. Then electricity replaced gas lamps. In time whole cities needed electricity. Power plants were built to supply electricity to great numbers of people. These stations converted energy sources—coal and oil— to electric power.

Gas lamp

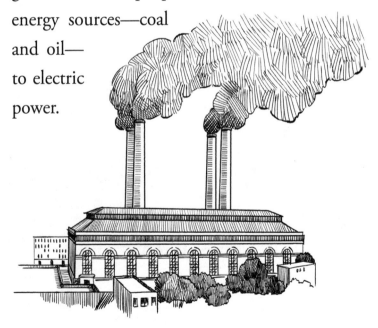

In homes, fireplaces were no longer needed to provide heat. Burners and furnaces were developed to keep houses warm. They used oil and gas.

Coal, oil, gas: All are fossil fuels. They're natural resources that come from long-buried plants and animals, ancient life forms that held carbon. When they're burned to generate power, they release the carbon as CO_2.

By the early 1900s, horses were traded in for cars. For long-distance travel, people took trains, and by the 1930s, flew in airplanes.

These forms of transportation burned coal or oil or ran on electricity from power plants. All needed fossil fuels. And all emitted CO_2.

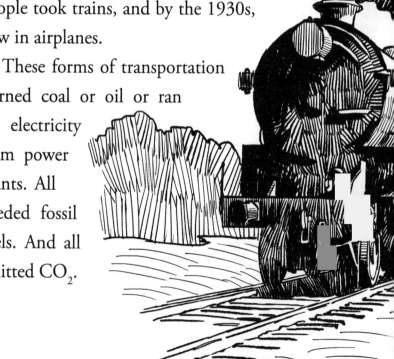

It's those CO_2 emissions—from factories and power plants, cars, trains, and airplanes—that send extra greenhouse gases into the atmosphere. Using fossil fuels creates "dirty energy," polluting the air with climate-changing gases.

"Clean energy," on the other hand, causes little emission pollution. And renewable energy has practically zero.

Renewable Energy

Energy from sources like wind, water, and the sun is called renewable energy because there is an endless supply of it. For solar energy, special glass panels capture the sun's power and convert it to electricity. Different kinds of turbines—windmill-like structures—use the wind or flowing water from rivers, streams, and waterfalls to spin blades and generate power. Unlike coal, oil, and gas, all these sources produce "clean" energy that doesn't pollute or emit greenhouse gases.

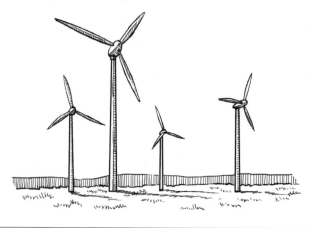

During the Industrial Revolution, and even afterward, no one thought about the amount of fossil fuel emissions. No one wondered if all that CO_2 would bring harmful consequences—not even scientists who knew about greenhouse gases.

As far back as the 1820s, scientists understood that CO_2 absorbed heat and helped keep the planet warm.

Then, in the 1890s, a Swedish scientist named Svante Arrhenius, along with his coworker Arvid Högbom, came up with a new idea. Could all the CO_2 that

Svante Arrhenius

came from factories be making a difference in temperature? Using math, Arrhenius came up with the first climate model, the first study to predict how temperature would rise with greater greenhouse gas emissions.

Other scientists studying the climate didn't think much of Arrhenius's findings. His model showed that if CO_2 increased 2.5–3 times the level it was then, temperatures in the Arctic would rise about 8–9°C (14.4–16.2°F). In other words, he argued that human-made CO_2 had a great influence on Earth's heat.

Other scientists questioned whether humans could have such an impact. The planet had been around for billions of years. Climate had changed before human beings ever existed. They thought that more greenhouse gas emissions might make temperatures go up. But just a bit. No big deal.

In addition, scientists had proven that oceans absorb CO_2. So wouldn't most of that extra gas be soaked right up by water?

But in the mid-1950s, an oceanographer named Roger Revelle ran some experiments and discovered that oceans have a limit to how much CO_2 they can take in. Also, they absorb it much more slowly than anyone had imagined. That meant temperature could rise quickly. In turn, rising temperature could change the delicate

Roger Revelle

balance of Earth's environment.

It became important to measure—and measure accurately—CO_2 levels in the atmosphere to see if Earth's climate was in danger.

CHAPTER 5
Measuring Up

Scientist Charles David Keeling of Scripps Institution of Oceanography helped develop ways to take those CO_2 measurements. He set up stations far away from cities and factories. He

Charles David Keeling

purposely didn't choose places near areas with higher-than-normal CO_2 levels. That would throw off the findings. One station was in the Antarctic, the other high on a volcano in Hawaii.

A New York City power plant from the early 1900s

View of Reid Glacier in Glacier Bay National Park, Alaska, 1956

View of Reid Glacier in Glacier Bay National Park, Alaska, 2013

A polar bear waits for the Hudson Bay to freeze over, 2007

Teenagers in an Alaskan village hopping onto melting sheets of ice

The Mauna Loa Observatory in Hawaii

The South Pole Observatory

The March for Science in Washington, DC, 2017

The first Earth Day event on the front page
of the New York *Daily News*, 1970

A woman paddles down a flooded road during the aftermath
of Hurricane Harvey in Texas, 2017

A young Kenyan boy stands on a dried-up riverbed, 2009

A raging wildfire in California, 2017

A bleached reef in the Great Barrier Reef, Australia, 2003

Workman at a natural gas plant, 1946

Wind turbines spin behind a field of solar cell panels in Germany

Mauna Loa Observatory

Built into the side of Mauna Loa volcano, this research center sits 11,135 feet (more than two miles) above sea level. It's the longest-running CO_2 measurement station in the world. Findings are plotted on "the Keeling Curve," a graph that has become a symbol of human impact on climate change. Daily measurements are posted on the observatory website. Check the bibliography in the back of the book to get the website link.

In 1958, the first results came in from both observatories. CO_2 levels stood at 310 ppm—parts per million. That means for every million bits of gas in the atmosphere, 310 of those bits were CO_2. In the 1700s, CO_2 levels had only been about 280 ppm.

The jump didn't seem too significant. It was far from an unsafe level. But what if it was a trend, and the levels kept rising?

The South Pole observatory closed. But Mauna Loa measured CO_2 levels year after year. Soon it became clear: The levels *were* rising ever higher.

Again, outside of Keeling's group and a small number of scientists, no one felt alarm.

In the early 1960s, scientists started using computers to predict Earth's climate in the future. Newer, more advanced models were developed over decades. To test them, scientists put in information about the atmosphere, rainfall, and other factors from past years (years that already had a climate record).

By the 2000s, the models proved accurate again and again. They not only predicted Earth's climate future, they explained Earth's climate past. And each model pinpointed greenhouse gases as the cause for recent warming.

In 2011, one model estimated that at least 74 percent of climate change since 1950 was due to human activity. Meanwhile, the global population had been growing steadily. So there were more

people who needed cars. More factories were needed to produce goods. Forests were cut down to make more living space.

By 2016, the CO_2 level hit 400 ppm. That was the highest it had been in four million years. The news made headlines.

Scientists realized warming was happening faster and faster.

Disappearing Rain Forests

Rain forests are thought to hold half of all the different life forms we have on Earth. But thousands and thousands of acres of forest are lost every day, threatening wildlife. Trees are cleared to make way for homes and farms, and also to provide wood. High temperatures and long dry periods destroy rain forests, too. All those downed trees release great amounts of CO_2 and no longer give off oxygen. That changes the carbon-cycle balance, further warming our climate.

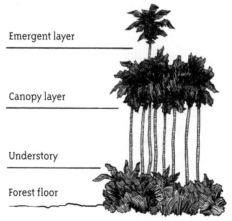

Emergent layer

Canopy layer

Understory

Forest floor

CHAPTER 6
Vicious Circles

Everything about the climate on Earth is connected. For instance, ocean currents affect air temperatures. Air temperatures affect plant life. Plant life affects the atmosphere. The atmosphere affects ocean currents. It comes full circle.

To put this idea in general terms: A makes a change in B, which in turn changes A, which changes B even more, and so on.

It becomes a vicious circle, a never-ending loop.

Melting ice and snow are one example. Ice and snow are clear and white. They act like mirrors, bouncing sunlight off their surfaces to keep Earth cool. But when temperatures rise, sea ice—along with land ice and snow—melts.

There is more open ocean and more uncovered land. Both are darker than snow and ice.

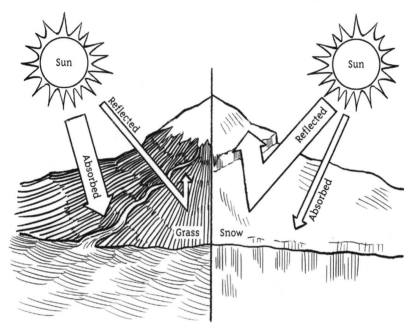

Have you noticed that when you wear a black shirt, you feel warmer in the sun than if you wear a white one? Dark colors soak up heat. So the darker ocean and land act like sponges, absorbing energy.

That extra energy warms Earth . . . which causes temperatures to rise . . . which melts more ice and snow . . . which exposes more ocean and land.

The effect is especially serious in the Arctic tundra, where permafrost is disappearing. The permafrost, which has been there for millions of years, holds methane. That is another greenhouse gas, one even stronger than CO_2. Methane doesn't stay in the atmosphere as long, but it traps about thirty times more heat.

When the permafrost melts, methane is released. The temperature goes up, and more permafrost melts, releasing more methane. And so on, and so on.

The more Earth warms, scientists realized, the quicker more warming occurs. In other words, higher temperatures lead to even higher temperatures.

It's one more factor in the science of climate change. But some people don't believe in the science.

They don't believe in climate change at all.

CHAPTER 7
Is It Real?

Scientists are always questioning their own findings, always exploring different possibilities, always retesting the results of experiments. How they investigate climate science is no exception.

So even climate scientists don't agree on all the details of global warming. That makes some people question *everything* climate scientists say they've proven. Some people even say climate change is a hoax. A lie. A trick. They think there is

no climate change—just weather, which changes as it always has.

Day to day, climate change *is* hard to see. Even if you're suffering through the middle of a heat wave, for instance, it could just be a bad stretch of natural weather.

It's true there have always been years with very severe heat waves. But with global warming, heat waves are more *likely* to happen and be worse than in years past. Warming may not be the cause of every event. But emitting more greenhouse gases increases the odds of extreme weather.

Almost all climate scientists agree on that and some other basic facts:

- Earth is heating up.
- It's because more and more greenhouse gases

are being released through fossil fuels into the atmosphere.

• People are responsible for this.

Still, to argue against the facts, some people bring up climate changes of the past. That Earth has always gone through cycles. During the Dinosaur Age, CO_2 levels were much, much higher. Some people believe that explains what is going on now. But remember, top scientists agree that given Earth's natural cycle, the planet should be cooling. They also say the sun is sending out less energy. Yet Earth is still warming.

Then there are some people who agree that, yes, human activity *is* causing the planet to warm, but they say that this is no cause for alarm. Plant life, animals, and humans can adapt to this climate change. After all, they have in the past.

However, those people are forgetting that earlier warming periods stretched over thousands and millions of years. Every form of life had time to change, to fit into a changing environment. Now warming is happening at a much faster rate.

Some people may accept all the science and even worry that Earth will not adapt to this current climate change. But, even though the warming is dangerous, they say it's not harmful *enough* for people to switch the way they use energy. People don't want to give up their modern lifestyles and also don't want to change to using clean energy instead of fossil fuels, which are

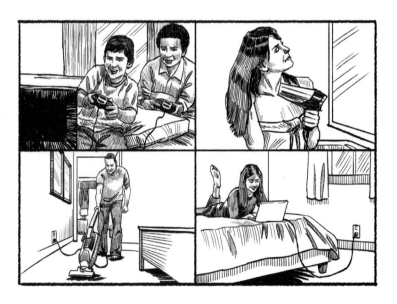

often less expensive. Certain businesses that rely on fossil fuels feel the same way. They don't want the government to pass laws limiting the release of CO_2.

So climate change isn't just a scientific issue. It's a political one, too.

CHAPTER 8
Politics

Fifty years ago in the United States, protecting the environment and preventing dangerous climate change was an issue everyone got behind. The two major political parties, Democrats and Republicans, took the same stand: Make Earth cleaner and greener.

In 1965, President Lyndon Baines Johnson announced, "This generation has altered the composition of the atmosphere on a global scale

Lyndon Baines Johnson

through . . . a steady increase in carbon dioxide from the burning of fossil fuels."

Richard Nixon

Johnson was a Democrat. The next president, Richard Nixon, was a Republican, and during his presidency, in 1970, Earth Day was established—a day to focus on protecting the planet.

That same year, the US government created the Environmental Protection Agency (EPA) to help protect human health and the environment. The Clean Air Act of 1970 was passed to control emissions and help air quality. Only one member of Congress voted against it.

The Environmental Protection Agency

The EPA helps set environmental policy. After Congress passes an environmental law, the EPA figures out the rules (regulations) needed to follow the new law. Climate change falls under the Clean Air Act of 1970. That allows the EPA to set emission limits on factories, cars, and more.

An environmental movement grew. Groups formed with the idea to protect the planet. Worldwide conferences were held, led by the United Nations, an international organization that works toward common goals among many countries.

The United Nations headquarters in New York City

At the very first UN environmental meeting in 1972, climate change gained attention. The focus was on air and water pollution. The group also warned governments to watch out for activities that could lead to warming.

Then, in the 1980s, scientists made a startling discovery. There was a huge hole in the protective layer of the atmosphere. Chemicals used in certain types of spray cans— like those for hair sprays—were destroying the ozone layer. (The ozone layer is part of the upper atmosphere and has a high level of the protective gas called ozone.) Without it, harmful sun rays could reach Earth.

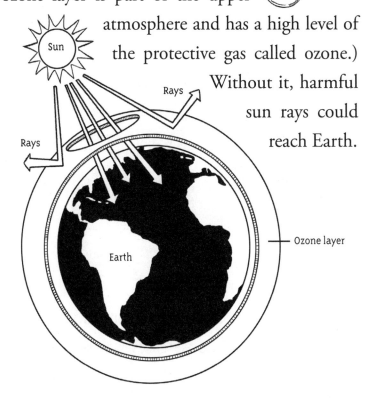

Sun

Rays

Rays

Ozone layer

Earth

President Ronald Reagan, a Republican, signed a treaty with dozens of other nations to ban the chemicals. The plan worked. The hole is closing.

At the same time, the concern about climate change was growing. In 1998, under Democratic president Bill Clinton, the United States signed an agreement called the Kyoto Protocol in Japan. Almost two hundred countries agreed to reduce emissions by at least 5 percent below 1990 levels.

In reality, however, little changed. Lowering the release of greenhouse gases was trickier than fixing the ozone layer. Also, the United States

Senate never ratified the agreement.

In the United States, many businesses—ones that made billions of dollars—counted on people to keep using fossil fuel energy: for example, oil companies, car manufacturers, and coal producers. If there were limits on releasing greenhouse gases, their businesses would suffer. People would be laid off from their jobs.

In the United States, certain groups within the Republican Party were on the side of these big businesses. So some politicians backed away from setting rules for company emissions. They said it was more important for people to keep their jobs and have the economy continue to grow.

Soon, people were taking sides along party lines. Ideas on climate change began to divide the country. By and large, Democrats were in favor of tougher laws to protect the environment while Republicans were against more regulation.

In 2001, Republican president George W. Bush formally pulled the United States out of the Kyoto Protocol. He claimed it would hurt the economy. Without the United States— one of the biggest energy users in the world—the Kyoto Protocol fell apart.

George W. Bush

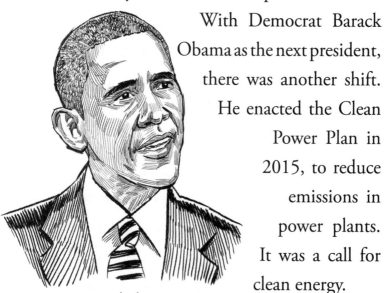

With Democrat Barack Obama as the next president, there was another shift. He enacted the Clean Power Plan in 2015, to reduce emissions in power plants. It was a call for clean energy.

Barack Obama

That same year, representatives of nearly two hundred countries met in Paris to discuss climate. Once again an agreement was signed. The agreement stated that all the countries would take steps to slow climate change and limit greenhouse gases, and they would try to do it by a certain year. The target for 2020: to stop global temperatures from rising any more than 3.6°F (2°C) higher than they'd been before the Industrial Revolution.

A picture of some representatives from the Paris Agreement

Donald Trump

Then, in 2017, there was yet another shift. The new US president, Donald Trump, who was a Republican, rolled back the Clean Power Plan. And at the end of May 2017, Trump announced the United States was pulling out of the Paris Agreement. In his speech, he stated concern about the country's economy and possible lost jobs. However, many big companies, such as Disney, Apple, and Google, said the job rate wouldn't be affected.

United States of America

Nicaragua

Even some energy companies urged the president to stay in. They thought it would mean big profits for their natural gas divisions. (Natural gas is a cleaner energy.)

And they might get government money to help them develop technology to reduce oil and coal pollution.

At first, two other countries—Syria and Nicaragua—did not join the agreement. But they later changed their positions, leaving the United States as the one country in the world not part of the Paris Agreement.

Syria

Well before the US withdrawal from the Paris Agreement, protests had been organized and rallies held all around the country. People who were worried about the future of Earth participated.

The March for Science was held on Earth Day in 2017. Hundreds of marches were held across the country, with the main one in Washington, DC. Scientists organized the marches to point out their role in helping the planet. They wanted to make sure that fact-based scientific studies of our world's environment continued.

Just days later, the EPA announced its website was "undergoing changes that reflect the agency's new direction under President Trump."

In the meantime, information about climate change was removed.

The announcement was followed, the very next day, by a series of already planned People's Climate Marches. The sole focus: climate change. Around two hundred thousand people from all over the country gathered for the main march in DC.

One high-school student went to the March for Science near his Boston home. Then he traveled to DC for the People's Climate March. "I wanted to deliver the climate facts directly to the center of government," he said later.

Why? "Because the risks are so great."

CHAPTER 9
Extreme Weather

As the temperature goes up, there are more frequent events of extreme weather. It's because the air has become warmer. Warm air "holds" more water than cold air. It contains more water molecules. It's damper, more humid, and more likely to turn into vapor. There's more water in the atmosphere. So when it rains, it rains a lot. In fact, there's a better chance it will pour. Floods have become more common.

The United States has seen this firsthand. Compared to fifty years ago, some areas have gotten about 67 percent more rainfall during the heaviest storms.

Heavy rains can destroy crops and homes. When these rains hit mountains, they can cause landslides and mudslides. Rivers flood. Bridges collapse. People may die.

With a warming planet, events like these are expected to happen more often.

In August 2016, two feet of rain fell in parts of Louisiana in just three days. Climate scientists took note. "The odds of an event like this have increased over the past one hundred years by at least 40 percent," said a Princeton University researcher who worked on one study. One year later, in August 2017, Hurricane Harvey dumped more than *four* feet of rain over parts of coastal Texas, setting a new record for the continental United States. No other storm had ever dropped so much rain!

Commenting on historic flooding in Peru, South America, in March 2017, the research director at the University of Colorado added this: "At four hundred ppm of CO_2 in the atmosphere . . . the question is not so much 'is this event caused by climate change?' The question is, 'which event is not?'"

So what about hurricanes? Are they connected to climate change?

The answer is still being debated.

In 2005, one of the deadliest hurricanes to ever strike US soil hit Gulf Coast states such as Mississippi, Louisiana, and Alabama. The city of New Orleans, Louisiana, was hit particularly hard by Hurricane Katrina. Waves of water poured into the streets, flooding 80 percent of the city.

Seven years later, Hurricane Sandy devastated the Northeast. Entire towns in New Jersey and New York were underwater.

Once again, the monster storms turned the nation's attention to global warming. Some studies say it's too early to tell if climate change was the main reason that those storms were so huge. Modern records only go back a few decades. So it's difficult to compare big storms of the past to more recent ones.

Some facts, though, are clear: Sea levels are rising. And higher sea levels cause major flood damage.

The Arctic Ocean is warmer. Ice melts, causing seas to rise. Plus, warm drops of water expand. They take up more space. With those

effects, global sea levels have gone up about eight inches over the past one hundred years.

During storms and hurricanes, heavy winds cause a storm surge, a sudden, powerful push of water onto land. With higher waters, the surge is greater. Water covers more land, doing more damage. Hurricane Sandy had a record storm surge—thirteen feet—in New York City. In regions near coasts, rising water levels mean higher daily tides and more flooding, too.

From 1998 to 2005, Miami Beach, Florida, had sixteen floods. From 2006 to 2013, there were thirty-three. More than twice as many.

Generally, regions that are already wet will get even wetter. But dry inland areas face other problems. And it's likely those problems will start with heat waves.

CHAPTER 10
Heat Waves

A heat wave is a period of days or weeks of unusually hot weather. With higher temperatures, it makes sense we'd have more heat waves and that they'd last longer.

In 2010, Russia experienced one of the worst heat waves on record. For the first time ever, temperatures reached 100°F there. Unused to those conditions and not prepared, about fifty-five thousand people died.

Experts from the National Center for Atmospheric Research and other institutions say if greenhouse gas emissions aren't curbed, the number of abnormally hot days could become much more frequent.

According to Dr. Michael E. Mann, the Distinguished Professor of Atmospheric Science at Penn State University, and Dr. Lee R. Kump, professor and head of the Department of Geosciences at Penn State, by the end of the century, St. Louis, Missouri, could have more than forty continuous days of brutal temperatures.

And more heat waves mean more droughts, long periods with very little rainfall.

It may seem strange that global warming can cause both droughts and floods. After all, they are opposite conditions. But remember, warm air holds more water. So in areas with little rain, high temperatures pull moisture from Earth's surface into the air.

These drops evaporate—disappear—
heat. So the air pulls even more moisture.
ground becomes dusty. Lakes and ponds dry up.

Think of a pot of water, boiling on a stove.
Water, in the form of steam, escapes into the air.
The water level goes down. Leave the burner on
too long and the water will disappear. Only a
burned pot is left—like parched, cracked ground.

California was in a drought from about 2012
to 2016. It was considered part of a fifteen-year
"megadrought" that lingered across most of the
western United States.

Lake Mead, a reservoir that provides much of California's water, shrank. In spring 2016, it dropped to a record low. It was just 37 percent full.

One study found that California could face permanent drought conditions by 2050—due in part to human-caused climate change.

The United States is not alone. Droughts have hit almost every continent. The consequences can be harsh. As in the Lake Chad region of Africa, there are water shortages . . . failing farms . . . loss of income . . .

And not enough food.

CHAPTER 11
Famine and Fire

Famine is a lack of food so great that people are in danger of dying.

In the African countries of Kenya, Somalia, Djibouti, and Ethiopia, famine goes hand in hand with droughts. Generally, the region has two rainy seasons each year. But when the rains don't come, drought follows. In 2011, the region was hit by the worst drought in six decades.

Soil grew sandy. Plants wilted. Farming was impossible. Food was scarce. Many families herded animals for a living. But the herds, like farmers, were in trouble. Without food or water, the animals were dying.

In Somalia and other countries, thousands of families left their homes in search of water. They traveled hundreds of miles. Some families made their way to refugee camps in northern Kenya, crowded spaces filled with others in need.

Some families split up. Outside the city of Garissa, Kenya, mothers with young children stayed in poor villages, gathering wood to sell for

pennies. Fathers kept walking with their herds, trying to find water. No one had enough to eat.

In July 2011, the United Nations declared a famine in Somalia. Between 2010 and 2012, about 260,000 people died, half of them young children. Just five years later, Somalis faced drought and famine conditions again.

"In the past, it was one big drought every ten years," said a director at World Vision, an organization that aids children and families. "Then it came to one drought every five years, and now the trends are showing that it will be one every three to five years. . . . We are in a crisis."

Climate change may not be causing every crisis. But it makes conditions more extreme. In dry areas, droughts and famines are more likely to happen. And in the American West, where there are vast forests, drought leads to a different kind of disaster: wildfires.

A warming climate means shorter winters and

longer, hotter summers. And during those long, hot summers, trees dry out. Like kindling, they catch fire quickly. And fire spreads faster.

Each year, raging wildfires sweep across states from California to Colorado. They start in forests, maybe from a lightning strike or campfire. Flames leap from tree to tree, shrub to shrub, jumping to grassy fields. Closer and closer to communities.

Wildfire season used to last five months. Now it can last more than seven months. Outbreaks have doubled and tripled.

In October 2017, California experienced its deadliest week for wildfires in state history. More than forty people died.

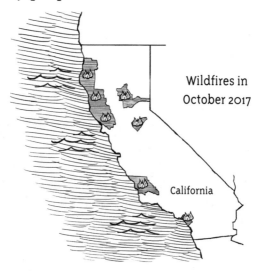

Wildfires in October 2017

California

As Mark Cochrane, a scientist from South Dakota State University, explained, "Ecosystems are designed to withstand the normal climate situation. But," he went on, "we suspect that things aren't normal anymore."

Danger: Bark Beetles!

Higher temperatures bring a beetle boom to forests. Bark beetles live inside trees, blocking water from traveling to branches. The trees dry out and die, becoming a fire hazard and sending more CO_2 into the air.

CHAPTER 12
Trouble at Sea

Oceans hold almost all our planet's water. They also hold a lot of CO_2. And that causes major consequences.

When CO_2 joins with seawater, it forms a kind of acid. A harsh chemical. It changes the water's very nature.

Sea creatures such as certain clams and oysters make their own shells. The shells help protect them. But with more acid in the water, the shells grow weak. They can even dissolve. Young clams and oysters die off. Entire species are at risk.

Krill in the Antarctic

In the warming Antarctic Ocean, krill—tiny shrimplike creatures—are in danger. Their life cycle is tied to water temperature, CO_2 levels, and how much seawater there is. With these factors changing, survival is difficult. Although climate change may not be the only cause, krill populations have dropped by 70 to 80 percent. Krill are a major food source for whales, seals, penguins, fish, and seabirds—some of which are food sources for other sea creatures. Without krill, the entire ecosystem is in danger.

The same holds true for bright, multicolored coral and coral reefs. Coral polyps (say: PAWL-lups) are sea animals, similar to jellyfish, found in tropical waters. As coral polyps grow, they produce limestone. This creates a hard coral skeleton, which grows and grows. Eventually, a coral reef builds up.

The Great Barrier Reef lies off the coast of Australia. It has almost three thousand reefs and hundreds of small islands. It teems with sea life: sponges, plants, and schools of colorful fish swimming in and out of hiding spots.

But the reef is in danger. Water chemistry is changing. And so is the water temperature. Over the last 135 years, the global sea surface temperature has gone up 1.1°F. Like most climate factors, a small change can make a big difference. And studies show that the most warming has happened most recently. It shows a trend.

When ocean water turns warm and acidic, coral feel stress. They lose their color and turn white. This is known as a "bleaching event." They grow weak and are more likely to die. In 2016, the reef experienced a bleaching. It was a great loss of life and color, with all its creatures endangered. Then it happened again in 2017. Two years in a row. That was unheard of. Everything was happening faster than expected.

Scientists predicted that by 2050, if CO_2 emissions didn't slow, the Great Barrier Reef would have bleaching events every year.

"The climate is changing," said an expert from the Great Barrier Marine Park Authority. "The overall impact of climate change is a major threat to the future of the reef."

This is the present. So what does the future look like?

CHAPTER 13
The Present and the Future

By the end of this century, oceans could be significantly warmer. Underwater habitats could be in even greater danger.

But what if emissions are greatly reduced?

Even then, sea levels would still rise a foot or two.

What if emissions aren't curbed? Sea levels could go up more than six feet.

But even with the lowest rise, regular tides could be more like "king tides." Those are the highest high tides of the year.

In Florida, steps are being taken to control flooding. Roads are being raised above sea level. Shopping malls are being built with protective barriers.

California, too, is thinking ahead. Some areas already have a system to recycle wastewater into tap water, to increase supplies.

From Florida to California. From polar bear habitats in the Arctic to coral reefs in Australia's Great Barrier Reef. Climate change is affecting entire regions.

In 2012, we were about two degrees away from the critically dangerous rise of 3.6°F. But since then we've had yearly record-breaking temperatures, and scientists are still figuring out the exact warming for the decade. One thing is for certain: If emissions keep increasing, their effects can get much worse.

However, it can work the other way, too. There's talk of charging companies money if they release dangerous emissions. Businesses won't want to pay a "carbon tax." So the hope is, they'd find another way to power their companies.

Some states have formed the United States Climate Alliance, pledging to still meet the Paris Agreement goals. California governor Jerry Brown even met with the president of China to discuss climate change.

And on June 6, 2017, Hawaii—a group of islands sure to be affected by rising seas—became the first state to sign greenhouse gas reductions into law.

It's a signal that our planet's dependence on fossil fuels can change.

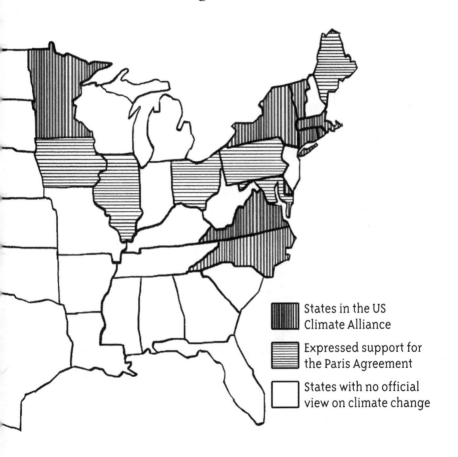

States in the US Climate Alliance

Expressed support for the Paris Agreement

States with no official view on climate change

Natural Gas and Nuclear Energy: Pros and Cons

Natural gas is a fossil fuel, drilled from deep beneath Earth's surface. It supplies about 30 percent of US energy and emits only about half as much CO_2 as coal does. But natural gas is mostly methane.

TVA Watts Bar
Nuclear Power Plant

Methane escapes during drilling and can leak from pipelines. One removal method, known as fracking, has been linked to earthquakes.

Nuclear reactors use the element uranium to produce energy. These power plants split the most basic unit of uranium, the atom, releasing energy from the nucleus, which is the atom's core. No greenhouse gases are emitted. But the process leaves toxic, poisonous waste and can cause health problems. Reactors can have "meltdowns," too, with uranium burning through the reactor and releasing harmful radiation into surrounding areas.

All over the world, people are already using renewable energy. Some sources generate power with zero or very light emissions—and they'll never be used up! Plus, renewable energy has become cheaper over time. It's a growing industry. In 2016, more Americans were employed in

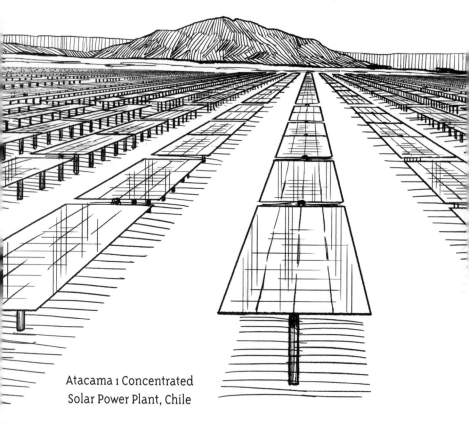

Atacama 1 Concentrated
Solar Power Plant, Chile

solar-energy work than in coal, gas, and oil jobs combined.

In rural areas of Africa, China, and India, solar panels are providing power to villages. Earlier, these areas couldn't connect to electric grids. Now people have refrigerators, lights, and more. It's changed lives.

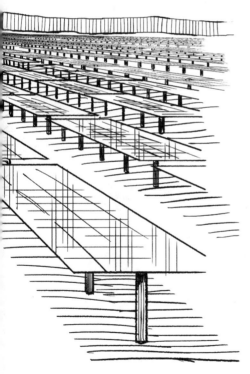

In Chile, a giant new solar power plant was built in a dry, sunny desert. It can provide electricity for one million people.

Solar panels are springing up in parking lots across the United States. They're set up as canopies above cars, protecting them from heat, rain, and snow.

Wind power is growing, too. More and more turbines are being built on farms. They can power one farm or many.

Everywhere, people are driving electric cars that don't burn fuel—or "hybrids" that use a mix of electricity and gas. Any kind of cycling saves energy. So does walking, taking a bus or train, or carpooling with friends. It means fewer vehicles on the road.

An electric car at a charging station

What can save energy at home? Special lightbulbs, called LED lights, use at least 75 percent less energy. And they last twenty-five times longer than regular bulbs. We all know that something as simple as turning off lights when you leave a room can help. Don't run water. Turn off the faucet while you brush your teeth.

Taking action helps reduce your "carbon footprint"—lowering how much CO_2 you produce. So what will be your impact on the environment? Do you believe that climate change presents a real danger in the immediate future to our planet? If so, what will you do about it?

Timeline of Climate Change

1790 — First factory built in Rhode Island, starting the American Industrial Revolution

1880 — Global temperature first measured for historical record

1896 — Svante Arrhenius publishes first model linking human CO_2 emissions to climate

1957 — Roger Revelle finds oceans have limited ability to absorb CO_2

1970 — Earth Day and the Environmental Protection Agency established

1972 — First United Nations environmental conference is held

1978 — Aerosol spray cans with CFCs banned around the world

1997 — Close to two hundred countries sign Kyoto Protocol to limit greenhouse gas emissions

2008 — US lists the polar bear as a threatened species at risk of becoming endangered due to habitat loss

2010 — Record-breaking heat wave in Russia, during which temperatures reach over 100°F

2011, 2015 — Drought in East African countries causes major famine

2016 — Annual global temperatures break record for third straight year

— CO_2 levels hit milestone of 400 ppm

2017 — President Trump rolls back the Clean Power Plan and pulls the US out of the 2015 Paris Agreement

Timeline of the World

1790 — President George Washington delivers first-ever State of the Union address on January 8

1896 — Leo Hirschfield invents the Tootsie Roll, named for his daughter

— First modern Olympic Games held in Athens, Greece

1903 — The first flight of the Wright brothers' powered airplane

1964 — President Lyndon Johnson signs the Civil Rights Act into law

1970 — Rock 'n' roll band the Beatles officially break up

1972 — First successful video game, *Pong*, debuts

1978 — Harriet Tubman becomes first African American woman honored on a US postage stamp

1997 — J. K. Rowling's first Harry Potter book, *Harry Potter and the Philosopher's Stone*, is published in the UK

2001 — Al-Qaeda terrorists highjack four airplanes, two of which destroy the Twin Towers at the World Trade Center in New York City

2009 — Barack Obama sworn in as first African American president of the United States

2010 — Apple introduces the iPad tablet computer

2016 — Donald Trump wins US presidential election

Bibliography

*Books for young readers

*Gore, Al. *An Inconvenient Truth: The Crisis of Global Warming*.
Young Readers Edition. New York: Viking, 2007.

Mann, Michael E., and Lee R. Kump. *Dire Predictions: Understanding Climate Change*. 2nd Edition. New York: DK Publishing, 2015.

*Medina, Nico. *What Was the Ice Age?* New York: Penguin Workshop, 2017.

Romm, Joseph. *Climate Change: What Everyone Needs to Know*.
New York: Oxford University Press, 2016.

*Woodward, John. *Eyewitness Books: Climate Change*. New York:
DK Publishing, 2008.

Websites

A Student's Guide to Global Climate Change. https://archive.epa.gov/climatechange/kids

Climate Kids: NASA's Eyes on the Earth. https://climatekids.nasa.gov

Mauna Loa Observatory: Trends in Atmospheric Carbon Dioxide.
www.esrl.noaa.gov/gmd/ccgg/trends/monthly.html

National Oceanic and Atmospheric Administration Climate Site.
www.noaa.gov/climate

National Ocean Service. www.oceanservice.noaa.gov

Ocean and Climate Change Institute, Woods Hole Oceanographic Institution. www.whoi.edu/main/occi

Sea Level Rise Viewer. https://coast.noaa.gov/slr